EGYPT PYRAMID COLOUR

MR VIVEK KUMAR PANDEY SHAMBHUNATH

ISBN 979-888555161-8

Short Information About Egypt Pyramid & Pyramids of Giza, three 4th-dynasty (c. 2575–c. 2465 BCE) pyramids erected on the west bank of the Nile River near Al-Jizah (Giza), northern Egypt.During writing this book no character & no religious are harmed written by Mr Vivek Kumar Pandey. winner youngest writer award 1st rank in india 2020.He is only one writer can publish 700+ own book that was greatest successfull in his life .This book fully colour edition books.

Contents

Foreword

Author biography in English :MY NAME IS VIVEK KUMAR PANDEY . I WAS BORN IN 30 SEP 2002,I AM FROM SURAT GUJARAT INDIA.MY DREAM WAS TO BE GOOD WRITERS ,MY FAMILY SUPPORTED ME TO SUCCESSFUL AND I CAN DO IT MY SELF.How do I write? That is a question, I believe, that can be honestly answered by me."CELEBRATING YOUNGEST WRITER AWARD WINNER IN GUJARAT 1ST RANK" MR PANDEY JI . I may think I did a good job writing something when in reality it could be horrible. The reader is the one who decides the quality of my writing. I do find writing to be natural to me and therefore find it to be a real challenge. My trick as a challenged writer is to do the best I can and know that I am happy with the final outcome. It may take a while to do my best and there may be quite a few problems I run into along the way.

I am not a greedy person those who are thinking about me and my self I never tried it anyone people suffering from sadness ,I trying to get promoted people suffering from happiness and joy in your Life Time. Now in current situation in India and also world people are unemployed and have no many but our indian governor help to people to get free food from ration card , i also take part in leadership team ,i am Motivational speaker , Film script writer. There was my two dream firstly writer and secondly actor & also my own film is upcoming soon i done almost completely completed script for my film .I AM GOING TO SAY WORD OF HEART TOUCH OUT PLEASE READ IT" , firstly i thanks my father he supports me in this field they always getting inspired me by own his words and behavior ,they always said that he was a biggest person in the world in future and also they purchase fruit and chocolate for me in anytime & anyway , firstly my father buy him then call me Vivek you want a chocolate i will say yes papa but how many tell me ,papa: you tell me how much i buy him i told 1 or 2 chocolate but my father purchase whole the boxes of chocolate and they get suprised me. MY FATHER WAS BORN IN " 20 SEPTEMBER" 1971 IN INDIA.

1) MY FATHER FAVORITE CLOTHES IS KURTA PAIJMA AND ALSO STYLES SHOE

2) FAVORITE SINGER IS KISHORE DA

3) FAVORITE STATE GUJARAT AND KOLKATA , HIS VILLAGE IN BIHAR

4) FAVORITE COLOR BLACK AND WHITE

THEY ALSO LOVE cricket like IPL and one day t-20 .they also like watching a News daily and heard the song daily ,they also interested in tik tok video but in current time tik tok is banned in india but also few videos are in you tube. In lockdown time my family and me very enjoy day daily. my father play daily ludo with his sister and son, daughter.they always loved tea and coffee anytime call me "। ववकि थोडा़ चाय बनाओना ववकि तमुहार ेहाथ का चाय अच्छा लगता हैं". I make it tea for my father but some reason after the April to june they are suffering from fever and cough , weakness on 6 June 2020 my father death. they not told me say bye bye his life. After death of 6 June on 10 june my mom and dad anniversary.but my father is Best in the world they can do anything for me please take care of father and respect it of your parents.

CHAPTER ONE

Egypt Pyramid Colour

- Egyptian pyramids

A view of the pyramids at Giza from the plateau to the south of the complex. From left to right, the three largest are: the Pyramid of Menkaure, the Pyramid of Khafre and the Great Pyramid of Khufu. The three smaller pyramids in the foreground are subsidiary structures associated with Menkaure's pyramid.

The Egyptian pyramids are ancient masonry structures located in Egypt. Sources cite at least 118 identified Egyptian pyramids. Most were built as tombs for the country's pharaohs and their consorts during the Old and Middle Kingdom periods.

The earliest known Egyptian pyramids are found at Saqqara, northwest of Memphis, although at least one step-pyramid-like structure has been found at Saqqara, dating to the First Dynasty: Mastaba 3808, which has been attributed to the reign of Pharaoh Anedjib, with inscriptions, and other archaeological remains of the period, suggesting there may have been others. The otherwise earliest among these is the Pyramid of Djoser built c. 2630–2610 BCE during the Third Dynasty. This pyramid and its surrounding complex are generally considered to be the world's oldest monumental structures constructed of dressed masonry.

The most famous Egyptian pyramids are those found at Giza, on the outskirts of Cairo. Several of the Giza pyramids are counted among the largest structures ever built.The Pyramid of Khufu is the largest Egyptian pyramid. It is the only one of the Seven Wonders of the Ancient World still in existence; this is despite being the oldest wonder by about 2,000 years.

- Egyptian pyramid

The name for a pyramid in Egyptian is myr. It is written with sign O24 of the Gardner Sign List. Myr is preceded by three other signs used as phonetics. The meaning of myr is unclear, as it only self-references the built object itself. By contrast architecture of similar function like 'temple‘, per-ka, is a compound of 'house‘ and 'soul'. It has been speculated myr belongs to a class of words like djed and ankh, which refer to objects already in existence when the Egyptian language split off from afroasiatic. A typical translation of myr is given as ‘High Place’. By graphical analysis, myr uses the same sign, O24, as benben. The benben is the mound of existence that rose of out of the abyss, nun, in the Egyptian creation myth. The relationship between myr and benben is further linked by the capstone architectural element of pyramids and obelisks, which was named benbenet, the feminine form of benben.

- Mastabat al-Fir'aun at Saqqara

The design of Egyptian pyramids, especially the stepped designs of the oldest pyramids (Pyramid of Zoser at Saqqara, 2600 BCE), may have been an evolution from the ziggurats built in Mesopotamia, dated to as early as 4000–3500 BCE.

Preceded by assumed earlier sites in the Eastern Sahara, tumuli with megalithic monuments developed as early as 4700 BCE in the Saharan region of Niger. It is also possible that these megalithic monuments in the Saharan region of Niger and the Eastern Sahara may have served as antecedents for the mastabas and pyramids of ancient Egypt. During Predynastic Egypt, tumuli were present at various locations (e.g., Naqada, Helwan).

From the time of the Early Dynastic Period (c. 3150–2686 BCE), Egyptians with sufficient means were buried in bench-like structures known as mastabas. At Saqqara, Mastaba 3808, dating from the latter part of the 1st Dynasty, was discovered to contain a large, independently built step-pyramid-like structure enclosed within the outer palace facade mastaba. Archaeological remains and inscriptions suggest there may have been other similar structures dating to this period.

The first historically documented Egyptian pyramid is attributed by Egyptologists to the 3rd Dynasty pharaoh Djoser. Although Egyptologists often credit his vizier Imhotep as its architect, the dynastic Egyptians themselves, contemporaneously or in numerous later dynastic writings about the character, did not credit him with either designing Djoser's pyramid or the invention of stone architecture. The Pyramid of Djoser was first built as a square mastaba-like structure, which as a rule were known to otherwise be rectangular, and was expanded several times by way of a series of accretion layers, to produce the stepped pyramid structure we see today.Egyptologists believe this design served as a gigantic stairway by which the soul of the deceased pharaoh could ascend to the heavens.

Though other pyramids were attempted in the 3rd Dynasty after Djoser, it was the 4th Dynasty, transitioning from the step pyramid to truc pyramid shape, which gave rise to the great pyramids of Meidum, Dahshur, and Giza. The last pharaoh of the 4th Dynasty, Shepseskaf, did not build a pyramid and beginning in the 5th Dynasty; for various reasons, the massive scale and precision of construction decreased significantly leaving these later pyramids smaller, less well-built, and often hastily constructed. By the end of the 6th Dynasty, pyramid building had largely ended and it was not until the Middle Kingdom that large pyramids were built again, though instead of stone, mudbrick was the main construction material.

Long after the end of Egypt's own pyramid-building period, a burst of pyramid-building occurred in what is present-day Sudan, after much of Egypt came under the rule of the Kingdom of Kush, which was then based at Napata. Napatan rule, known as the 25th Dynasty, lasted from 750 BCE to 664 BCE. The Meroitic period of Kushite history, when the kingdom was centered on Meroë, (approximately in the period between 300 BCE and 300 CE), experienced a full-blown pyramid-building revival, which saw about 180 Egyptian-inspired indigenous royal pyramid-tombs constructed in the vicinity of the kingdom's capital cities.

Al-Aziz Uthman (1171–1198), the second Ayyubid Sultan of Egypt, tried to destroy the Giza pyramid complex. He gave up after only damaging the Pyramid of Menkaure because the task proved too large.

- Pyramid symbolism

Diagram of the interior structures of the Great Pyramid. The inner line indicates the pyramid's present profile, the outer line indicates the original profile.

The shape of Egyptian pyramids is thought to represent the primordial mound from which the Egyptians believed the earth was created. The shape of a pyramid is also thought to be representative of the descending rays of the sun, and most pyramids were faced with polished, highly reflective white limestone, in order to give them a brilliant appearance when viewed from a distance. Pyramids were often also named in ways that referred to solar luminescence. For example, the formal name of the Bent Pyramid at Dahshur was The Southern Shining Pyramid, and that of Senusret II at El Lahun was Senusret Shines.

While it is generally agreed that pyramids were burial monuments, there is continued disagreement on the particular theological principles that might have given rise to them. One suggestion is that they were designed as a type of "resurrection machine."

The Egyptians believed the dark area of the night sky around which the stars appear to revolve was the physical gateway into the heavens. One of the narrow shafts that extend from the main burial chamber through the entire body of the Great Pyramid points directly towards the center of this part of the sky. This suggests the pyramid may have been designed to serve as a means to magically launch the deceased pharaoh's soul directly into the abode of the gods.

All Egyptian pyramids were built on the west bank of the Nile, which, as the site of the setting sun, was associated with the realm of the dead in Egyptian mythology.

- Number and location of pyramids

In 1842, Karl Richard Lepsius produced the first modern list of pyramids—now known as the Lepsius list of pyramids—in which he counted 67. A great many more have since been discovered. At least 118 Egyptian pyramids have been identified. The location of Pyramid 29 which Lepsius called the "Headless Pyramid", was lost for a second time when the structure was buried by desert sands after Lepsius's survey. It was found again only during an archaeological dig conducted in 2008.

Many pyramids are in a poor state of preservation or buried by desert sands. If visible at all, they may appear as little more than mounds of rubble. As a consequence, archaeologists are continuing to identify and study previously unknown pyramid structures.

The most recent pyramid to be discovered was that of Sesheshet at Saqqara, mother of the Sixth Dynasty pharaoh Teti, announced on 11 November 2008.

All of Egypt's pyramids, except the small Third Dynasty pyramid at Zawyet el-Maiyitin, are sited on the west bank of the Nile, and most are grouped together in a number of pyramid fields. The most important of these are listed geographically, from north to south, below.

- Abu Rawash

The largely destroyed Pyramid of Djedefre

Abu Rawash is the site of Egypt's most northerly pyramid (other than the ruins of Lepsius pyramid number one), the mostly ruined Pyramid of Djedefre, son and successor of Khufu. Originally it was thought that this pyramid had never been completed, but the current archaeological consensus is that not only was it completed, but that it was originally about the same size as the Pyramid of Menkaure, which would have placed it among the half-dozen or so largest pyramids in Egypt.

Its location adjacent to a major crossroads made it an easy source of stone. Quarrying, which began in Roman times, has left little apart from about fifteen courses of stone superimposed upon the natural hillock that formed part of the pyramid's core. A small adjacent satellite pyramid is in a better state of preservation.

- Giza

The Giza Plateau is the location of the Pyramid of Khufu (also known as the "Great Pyramid" and the "Pyramid of Cheops"), the somewhat smaller Pyramid of Khafre (or Chephren), the relatively modest-sized Pyramid of Menkaure (or Mykerinus), along with a number of smaller satellite edifices known as "Queen's pyramids", and the Great Sphinx of Giza. Of the three, only Khafre's pyramid retains part of its original polished limestone casing, near its apex. This pyramid appears larger than the adjacent Khufu pyramid by virtue of its more elevated location, and the steeper angle of inclination of its construction—it is, in fact, smaller in both height and volume.

The Giza pyramid complex has been a popular tourist destination since antiquity and was popularized in Hellenistic times when the Great Pyramid was listed by Antipater of Sidon as one of the Seven Wonders of the Ancient World. Today it is the only one of those wonders still in existence.

- Zawyet el-Aryan

This site, halfway between Giza and Abusir, is the location for two unfinished Old Kingdom pyramids. The northern structure's owner is believed to be pharaoh Nebka, while the southern structure, known as the Layer Pyramid, may be attributable to the Third Dynasty pharaoh Khaba, a close successor of Sekhemkhet. If this attribution is correct, Khaba's short reign could explain the seemingly unfinished state of this step pyramid. Today it stands around 17 m (56 ft) high; had it been completed, it is likely to have exceeded 40 m (130 ft).

- Abusir

The Pyramid of Sahure at Abusir, viewed from the pyramid's causeway

There are a total of fourteen pyramids at this site, which served as the main royal necropolis during the Fifth Dynasty. The quality of construction of the Abusir pyramids is inferior to those of the Fourth Dynasty—perhaps signaling a decrease in royal power or a less vibrant economy. They are smaller than their predecessors and are built of low-quality local limestone.

The three major pyramids are those of Niuserre, which is also the best-preserved, Neferirkare Kakai and Sahure. The site is also home to the incomplete Pyramid of Neferefre. Most of the major pyramids at Abusir were built using similar construction techniques, comprising a rubble core surrounded by steps of mudbricks with a limestone outer casing. The largest of these Fifth Dynasty pyramids, the Pyramid of Neferirkare Kakai, is believed to have been built originally as a step pyramid some 70 m (230 ft) high and then later transformed into a "true" pyramid by having its steps filled in with loose masonry.

- Saqqara

The Pyramid of Djoser

Major pyramids located here include the Pyramid of Djoser—generally identified as the world's oldest substantial monumental structure to be built of dressed stone—the Pyramid of Userkaf, the Pyramid of Teti and the Pyramid of Merikare, dating to the First Intermediate Period of Egypt. Also at Saqqara is the Pyramid of Unas, which retains a pyramid causeway that is one of the best-preserved in Egypt. Together with the pyramid of Userkaf, this pyramid was the subject of one of the earliest known restoration attempts, conducted by Khaemweset, a son of Ramesses II.

Saqqara is also the location of the incomplete step pyramid of Djoser's successor Sekhemkhet, known as the Buried Pyramid. Archaeologists believe that had this pyramid been completed, it would have been larger than Djoser's.

South of the main pyramid field at Saqqara is a second collection of later, smaller pyramids, including those of Pepi I, Djedkare Isesi, Merenre, Pepi II and Ibi. Most of these are in a poor state of preservation.

The Fourth Dynasty pharaoh Shepseskaf either did not share an interest in or have the capacity to undertake pyramid construction like his predecessors. His tomb, which is also sited at south Saqqara, was instead built as an unusually large mastaba and offering temple complex. It is commonly known as the Mastabat al-Fir'aun.

A previously unknown pyramid was discovered in north Saqqara in late 2008. Believed to be the tomb of Teti's mother, it currently stands approximately 5 m (16 ft) high, although the original height was closer to 14 m (46 ft).

- Dahshur

Sneferu's Red Pyramid

This area is arguably the most important pyramid field in Egypt outside Giza and Saqqara, although until 1996 the site was inaccessible due to its location within a military base and was relatively unknown outside archaeological circles.

The southern Pyramid of Sneferu, commonly known as the Bent Pyramid, is believed to be the first Egyptian pyramid intended by its builders to be a "true" smooth-sided pyramid from the outset; the earlier pyramid at Meidum had smooth sides in its finished state, but it was conceived and built as a step pyramid, before having its steps filled in and concealed beneath a smooth outer casing of dressed stone. As a true smooth-sided structure, the Bent Pyramid was only a partial success—albeit a unique, visually imposing one; it is also the only major Egyptian pyramid to retain a significant proportion of its original smooth outer limestone casing intact. As such it serves as the best contemporary example of how the ancient Egyptians intended their pyramids to look. Several kilometres to the north of the Bent Pyramid is the last—and most successful—of the three pyramids constructed during the reign of Sneferu; the Red Pyramid is the world's first successfully completed smooth-sided pyramid. The structure is also the third-largest pyramid in Egypt, after the pyramids of Khufu and Khafra at Giza.

Also at Dahshur is one of two pyramids built by Amenemhat III, known as the Black Pyramid, as well as a number of small, mostly ruined subsidiary pyramids.

- Mazghuna

Located to the south of Dahshur, several mudbrick pyramids were built in this area in the late Middle Kingdom, perhaps for Amenemhat IV and Sobekneferu.

- The Pyramid of Amenemhet I at Lisht

Lisht

Two major pyramids are known to have been built at Lisht: those of Amenemhat I and his son, Senusret I. The latter is surrounded by the ruins of ten smaller subsidiary pyramids. One of these subsidiary pyramids is known to be that of Amenemhat's cousin, Khaba II. The site which is in the vicinity of the oasis of the Faiyum, midway between Dahshur and Meidum, and about 100 kilometres south of Cairo, is believed to be in the vicinity of the ancient city of Itjtawy (the precise location of which remains unknown), which served as the capital of Egypt during the Twelfth Dynasty.

- Meidum

The pyramid at Meidum

The pyramid at Meidum is one of three constructed during the reign of Sneferu, and is believed by some to have been started by that pharaoh's father and predecessor, Huni. However, that attribution is uncertain, as no record of Huni's name has been found at the site. It was constructed as a step pyramid and then later converted into the first "true" smooth-sided pyramid, when the steps were filled in and an outer casing added. The pyramid suffered several catastrophic collapses in ancient and medieval times. Medieval Arab writers described it as having seven steps, although today only the three uppermost of these remain, giving the structure its odd, tower-like appearance. The hill on which the pyramid is situated is not a natural landscape feature, it is the small mountain of debris created when the lower courses and outer casing of the pyramid gave way.

- Hawara

The Pyramid of Amenemhet III at Hawara

Amenemhat III was the last powerful ruler of the Twelfth Dynasty, and the pyramid he built at Hawara, near the Faiyum, is believed to post-date the so-called "Black Pyramid" built by the same ruler at Dahshur. It is the Hawara pyramid that is believed to have been Amenemhet's final resting place.

- El Lahun

The Pyramid of Senusret II. The pyramid's natural limestone core is clearly visible as the yellow stratum at its base.The Pyramid of Senusret II at El Lahun is the southernmost royal-tomb pyramid structure in Egypt. Its builders reduced the amount of work necessary to construct it by using as its foundation and core a 12-meter-high natural limestone hill.

- El-Kurru

Piye's pyramid at El-Kurru

Piye, the king of Kush who became the first ruler of the Twenty-fifth Dynasty, built a pyramid at El-Kurru. He was the first Egyptian pharaoh to be buried in a pyramid in centuries.

- Nuri

Taharqa's pyramid at Nuri

Taharqa, a Kushite ruler of the Twenty-fifth Dynasty, built his pyramid at Nuri. It was the largest in the area (North Sudan).

Pyramidion

- Pyramidion

Pyramidion from the tomb of the priest Rer in Abydos, Egypt. Hermitage Museum

A pyramidion is the uppermost piece or capstone of an Egyptian pyramid or obelisk. Speakers of the Ancient Egyptian language referred to pyramidia as benbenetand associated the pyramid as a whole with the sacred benben stone. During Egypt's Old Kingdom, pyramidia were generally made of diorite, granite, or fine limestone, then covered in gold or electrum; during the Middle Kingdom and through the end of the pyramid-building era, they were built from granite. A pyramidion was "covered in gold leaf to reflect the rays of the sun"; during Egypt's Middle Kingdom pyramidia were often "inscribed with royal titles and religious symbols".

Very few pyramidia have survived into modern times. Most of those that remain are made of polished black granite, inscribed with the name of the pyramid's owner. Four pyramidia – the world's largest collection – are housed in the main hall of the Egyptian Museum in Cairo. Among them are the pyramidia from the so-called Black Pyramid of Amenemhat III at Dahshur and of the Pyramid of Khendjer at Saqqara.

A badly damaged white Tura limestone pyramidion, thought to have been made for the Red Pyramid of Sneferu at Dahshur, has been reconstructed and is on open-air display beside that pyramid; it presents a minor mystery, however, as its angle of inclination is steeper than that of the edifice it was apparently built to surmount.

- Private brick pyramids with pyramidia

During the New Kingdom, some private underground tombs were marked on the surface by small brick pyramids that terminated in pyramidia. The four lateral sides included texts and scenes related to the cult of the Sun

God.

The scenes typically depict the course of the sun, rising on one lateral face, setting on the opposite face, and traveling, through the night, through the underworld, ruled by Osiris.

- Egyptian hieroglyphs

The pyramidion of Mose (mes,s, New Kingdom, 19th Dynasty, c. 1250 BC, limestone, 53 cm tall) depicts himself making an offering, with his name on two opposite faces. The adjacent opposite faces feature a baboon: "Screeching upon the rising of the Sun, and the Day". (The baboon is also the god-scribe representation of the Scribe, for the god Thoth.)

- Ptahemwia pyramidion

The pyramidion of Ptahemwia (19th Dynasty, Ramesside Period, c. 1200 BC, limestone, 28 cm wide, 42 cm tall) likewise displays sun-related scenes.The Sun God, Re-Horakhti, and the god of the Underworld, Osiris, are shown on one lateral face.

Facing the two gods, on the adjacent lateral face, is the deceased Ptahemwia, standing in an offering pose, facing three columns of hieroglyphs.

CHAPTER TWO

Great Pyramid of Giza

1. Great Pyramid of Giza

Inscription1979 (3rd Session)

The Great Pyramid of Giza (also known as the Pyramid of Khufu or the Pyramid of Cheops) is the oldest and largest of the pyramids in the Giza pyramid complex bordering present-day Giza in Greater Cairo, Egypt. It is the oldest of the Seven Wonders of the Ancient World, and the only one to remain largely intact.

Egyptologists conclude that the pyramid was built as a tomb for the Fourth Dynasty Egyptian pharaoh Khufu and estimate that it was built in the 26th century BC during a period of around 27 years.

Initially standing at 146.5 metres (481 feet), the Great Pyramid was the tallest man-made structure in the world for more than 3,800 years. Throughout history the majority of the smooth white limestone casing was removed, which lowered the pyramid's height to the present 138.5 metres (454.4 ft). What is seen today is the underlying core structure. The base was measured to be about 230.3 metres (755.6 ft) square, giving a volume of roughly 2.6 million cubic metres (92 million cubic feet), which includes an internal hillock.

The dimensions of the pyramid were 280 royal cubits (146.7 m; 481.4 ft) high, a base length of 440 cubits (230.6 m; 756.4 ft)

The Great Pyramid was built by quarrying an estimated 2.3 million large blocks weighing 6 million tonnes total. The majority of stones are not uniform in size or shape and are only roughly dressed.The outside layers were bound together by mortar. Primarily local limestone from the Giza Plateau was used. Other blocks were imported by boat down the Nile: White limestone from Tura for the casing, and granite blocks from Aswan, weighing up to 80 tonnes, for the King's Chamber structure.

There are three known chambers inside the Great Pyramid. The lowest was cut into the bedrock, upon which the pyramid was built, but remained unfinished. The so-called Queen's Chamber and King's Chamber, that contains a granite sarcophagus, are higher up, within the pyramid structure. Khufu's vizier, Hemiunu (also called Hemon), is believed by some to be the architect of the Great Pyramid. Many varying scientific and alternative hypotheses attempt to explain the exact construction techniques.

The funerary complex around the pyramid consisted of two mortuary temples connected by a causeway (one close to the pyramid and one near the Nile), tombs for the immediate family and court of Khufu, including three smaller pyramids for Khufu's wives, an even smaller "satellite pyramid" and five buried solar barges.

1. Attribution to Khufu

Clay seal bearing the name of Khufu from the Great Pyramid on display at the Louvre museum

Khufu's cartouche found inscribed on a backing stone of the pyramid.

Historically the Great Pyramid had been attributed to Khufu based on the words of authors of classical antiquity, first and foremost Herodotus and Diodorus Siculus. However, during the middle ages a number of other people were credited with the construction of the pyramid as well, for example Josef, Nimrod or king Saurid.

In 1837 four additional Relieving Chambers were found above the King's Chamber after tunneling to them. The chambers, previously inaccessible, were covered in hieroglyphs of red paint. The workers who were building the pyramid had marked the blocks with the names of their gangs, which included the pharaoh's name (e.g.: "The gang, The white crown of Khnum-Khufu is powerful"). The names of Khufu were spelled out on the walls over a dozen times. Another of these graffiti was found by Goyon on an exterior block of the 4th layer of the pyramid.The inscriptions are comparable to those found at other sites of Khufu, such as the alabaster quarry at Hatnubor the harbor at Wadi al-Jarf, and are present in pyramids of other pharaohs as well.

- Throughout the 20th century the cemeteries next to the pyramid were excavated. Family members and high officials of Khufu were buried in the East Field south of the causeway, and the West Field. Most notably the wives, children and grandchildren of Khufu, Hemiunu, Ankhaf and (the funerary cache of) Hetepheres I, mother of Khufu. As Hassan puts it: "From the early dynastic times, it was always the custom for the relatives, friends and courtiers to be buried in the vicinity of the king they had served during life. This was quite in accordance with the Egyptian idea of the Hereafter."

The cemeteries were actively expanded until the 6th dynasty and used less frequently afterwards. The earliest pharaonic name of seal impressions is that of Khufu, the latest of Pepi II. Worker graffiti was written on some of the stones of the tombs as well; for instance, "Mddw" (Horus name of Khufu) on the mastaba of Chufunacht, probably a grandson of Khufu.

- Some inscriptions in the chapels of the mastabas (like the pyramid, their burial chambers were usually bare of inscriptions) mention Khufu or his pyramid. For instance, an inscription of Mersyankh III states that "Her mother daughter of the King of Upper and Lower Egypt Khufu." Most often these references are part of a title, for example, Snnw-ka, "Chief of the Settlement and Overseer of the Pyramid City of Akhet-Khufu" or Merib, "Priest of Khufu". Several tomb owners have a king's name as part of their own name (e.g. Chufudjedef, Chufuseneb, Merichufu). The earliest pharaoh alluded to in that manner at Giza is Snefru (Khufu's father).

In 1936 Hassan uncovered a stela of Amenhopet II near the Great Sphinx of Giza which implies the two larger pyramids were still attributed to Khufu and Khafre in the New Kingdom. It reads: "He yoked the horses in Memphis, when he was still young, and stopped at the Sanctuary of Hor-em-akhet (the Sphinx). He spent a time there in going round it, looking at the beauty of the Sanctuary of Khufu and Khafra the revered."

In 1954 two boat pits, one containing the Khufu ship, were discovered buried at the south foot of the pyramid. The cartouche of Djedefre was found on many of the blocks that covered the boat pits. As the successor and eldest son he would have presumably been responsible for the burial of Khufu. The second boat pit was examined in 1987; excavation work started in 2010. Graffiti on the stones included 4 instances of the name "Khufu", 11 instances of "Djedefre", a year (in reign, season, month and day), measurements of the stone, various signs and marks, and a reference line used in construction, all done in red or black ink.

During excavations in 2013 the Diary of Merer was found at Wadi al-Jarf. It documents the transportation of white limestone blocks from Tura to the Great Pyramid, which is mentioned by its original name Akhet Khufu (with a pyramid determinative) dozens of times. It details that the stones were accepted at She Akhet-Khufu ("the pool of the pyramid Horizon of Khufu") and Ro-She Khufu (“the entrance to the pool of Khufu”) which were under supervision of Ankhhaf, half brother and vizier of Khufu, as well as owner of the largest mastaba of the Giza East Field.

The Great Pyramid has been determined to be about 4600 years old by two principal approaches: indirectly, through its attribution to Khufu and his chronological age, based on archaeological and textual evidence; and directly, via radiocarbon dating of organic material found in the pyramid and included in its mortar.

1. Egyptian chronology

In the past the Great Pyramid was dated by its attribution to Khufu alone, putting the construction of the Great Pyramid within his reign. Hence dating the pyramid was a matter of dating Khufu and the 4th dynasty. The relative sequence and synchronicity of events stands at the focal point of this method.

- Absolute calendar dates are derived from an interlocked network of evidence, the backbone of which are the lines of succession known from ancient king lists and other texts. The reign lengths from Khufu to known points in the earlier past are summated, bolstered with genealogical data, astronomical observations, and other sources. As such, the historical chronology of Egypt is primarily a political chronology, thus independent from other types of archaeological evidence like stratigraphies, material culture, or radiocarbon dating.

The majority of recent chronological estimates date Khufu and his pyramid roughly between 2700 and 2500 BC.

- Radiocarbon dating

Mortar was used generously in the Great Pyramid's construction. In the mixing process ashes from fires were added to the mortar, organic material that could be extracted and radiocarbon dated. A total of 46 samples of the mortar were taken in 1984 and 1995, making sure they were clearly inherent to the original structure and could not have been incorporated at a later date. The results were calibrated to 2871–2604 BC. The old wood problem is thought to be mainly responsible for the 100–300 year offset, since the age of the organic material was determined, not when it was last used. A reanalysis of the data gave a completion date for the pyramid between 2620 and 2484 BC, based on the younger samples.

In 1872 Waynman Dixon opened the lower pair of "Air-Shafts", previously closed at both ends, by chiseling holes into the walls of the Queen's Chamber. One of the objects found within was a cedar plank, which came into possession of James Grant, a friend of Dixon. After inheritance it was donated to the Museum of Aberdeen in 1946, however it had broken into pieces and was filed incorrectly. Lost in the vast museum collection, it was only rediscovered in 2020, when it was radiocarbon dated to 3341–3094 BC. Being over 500 years older than Khufu's chronological age, Abeer Eladany suggests that the wood originated from the center of a long-lived tree or had been recycled for many years prior to being deposited in the pyramid.

1. History of dating Khufu and the Great Pyramid

Circa 450 BC Herodotus attributed the Great Pyramid to Cheops (Hellenization of Khufu), yet erroneously placed his reign following the Ramesside period. Manetho, around 200 years later, composed an extensive list of Egyptian kings which he divided into dynasties, assigning Khufu to the 4th. However, after phonetic changes in the Egyptian language and consequently the Greek translation, "Cheops" had transformed into "Souphis" (and similar versions).

- Greaves, in 1646, reported the great difficulty of ascertaining a date for the pyramid's construction based on the lacking and conflicting historic sources. Because of the aforementioned differences in spelling, he didn't recognize Khufu on Manetho's king list (as transcribed by Africanus and Eusebius), hence he relied on Herodotus' incorrect account. Summating the duration of lines of succession, Greaves concluded the year 1266 BC to be the beginning of Khufu's reign.

Two centuries later, some of the gaps and uncertainties in Manetho's chronology had been cleared by discoveries such as the King Lists of Turin, Abydos, and Karnak. The names of Khufu found within the Great Pyramid's Relieving Chambers in 1837 helped to make clear that Cheops and Souphis are, in fact, one and the same. Thus the Great Pyramid was recognized to have been built in the 4th dynasty. The dating among Egyptologists still varied by multiple centuries (around 4000–2000 BC), depending on methodology, preconceived religious notions (such as the biblical deluge) and which source they thought was more credible.

- Estimates significantly narrowed in the 20th century, most being within 250 years of each other, around the middle of the third millennium BC. The newly developed radiocarbon dating method confirmed that the historic chronology was approximately correct. It is, however, still not a fully appreciated method due to larger margins or error, calibration uncertainties and the problem of inbuilt age (time between growth and final usage) in plant material, including wood.Furthermore, astronomical alignments have been suggested to coincide with the time of construction.

Egyptian chronology continues to be refined and data from multiple disciplines have started to be factored in, such as luminescence dating, radiocarbon dating, and dendrochronology. For instance, Ramsey et al. included over 200 radiocarbon samples in their model.

- The Greek historian Herodotus was one of the first major authors to discuss the Great Pyramid

The ancient Greek historian Herodotus, writing in the 5th century BC, is one of the first major authors to mention the pyramid. In the second book of his work The Histories, he discusses the history of Egypt and the Great Pyramid. This report was created more than 2000 years after the structure was built, meaning that Herodotus obtained his knowledge mainly from a variety of indirect sources, including officials and priests of low rank, local Egyptians, Greek immigrants, and Herodotus's own interpreters. Accordingly, his explanations present themselves as a mixture of comprehensible descriptions, personal descriptions, erroneous reports, and fantastical legends; as such, many of the speculative errors and confusions about the monument can be traced back to Herodotus and his work.

Herodotus writes that the Great Pyramid was built by Khufu who, he erroneously relays, ruled after the Ramesside Period (Dynasties XIX and XX). Khufu was a tyrannical king, Herodotus claims, which may explain the Greek's view that such buildings can only come about through cruel exploitation of the people. Herodotus further states that gangs of 100,000 labourers worked on the building in three-month shifts, taking 20 years to build. In the first ten years a wide causeway was erected, which, according to Herodotus, was almost as impressive as the construction of the pyramids themselves. It measured nearly 1 kilometre (0.62 mi) long and 20 yards (18.3 m) wide, and elevated to a height of 16 yards (14.6 m), consisting of stone polished and carved with figures. In addition, underground chambers were made on the hill whereon the pyramids stand. These were intended to be burial places for Khufu himself and were encompassed with water by a channel brought in from the Nile. Herodotus later states that at the Pyramid of Khafre (located beside the Great Pyramid) the Nile flows through a built passage to an island in which Khufu is buried. (Hawass interprets this to be a reference to the "Osiris Shaft" which is located at the causeway of Khafre, south of the Great Pyramid.)

Herodotus also described an inscription on the outside of the pyramid which, according to his translators, indicated the amount of radishes, garlic and onions that the workers would have eaten while working on the pyramid. This could be a note of restoration work that Khaemweset, son of Rameses II, had carried out. Apparently, Herodotus companions and interpreters could not read the hieroglyphs or deliberately gave him false information.

- Diodorus Siculus

Between 60–56 BC, the ancient Greek historian Diodorus Siculus visited Egypt and later dedicated the first book of his Bibliotheca historica to the land, its history, and its monuments, including the Great Pyramid. Diodorus's work was inspired by historians of the past, but he also distanced himself from Herodotus, who Diodorus claims tells marvelous tales and myths. Diodorus presumably drew his knowledge from the lost work of Hecataeus of Abdera, and like Herodotus, he also places the builder of the pyramid, "Chemmis,"after Ramses III. According to his report, neither Chemmis (Khufu) nor Cephren (Khafre) were buried in their pyramids, but rather in secret places, for fear that the people ostensibly forced to build the structures would seek out the bodies for revenge with this assertion, Diodorus strengthened the connection between pyramid building and slavery.

According to Diodorus, the cladding of the pyramid was still in excellent condition at the time, whereas the uppermost part of the pyramid was formed by a platform 6 cubits (3.1 m; 10.3 ft) high. About the construction of the pyramid he notes that it was built with the help of ramps since no lifting tools had yet been invented. Nothing was left of the ramps, as they were removed after the pyramids were completed. He estimated the number of workers necessary to erect the Great Pyramid at 360,000 and the construction time at 20 years. Similar to Herodotus, Diodorus also claims that the side of the pyramid is inscribed with writing that "forth vegetables and purgatives for the workmen there were paid out over sixteen hundred talents."

- Strabo

The Greek geographer, philosopher, and historian Strabo visited Egypt around 25 BC, shortly after Egypt was annexed by the Romans. In his work Geographica, he argues that the pyramids were the burial place of kings, but he does not mention which king was buried in the structure. Strabo also mentions: "At a moderate height in one of the sides is a stone, which may be taken out; when that is removed, there is an oblique passage to the tomb."This statement has generated much speculation, as it suggests that the pyramid could be entered at this time.

- Pliny the Elder

During the Roman Empire, Pliny the Elder argues that "bridges" were used to transport stones to the top of the Great Pyramid..

The Roman writer Pliny the Elder, writing in the first century AD, argued that the Great Pyramid had been raised, either "to prevent the lower classes from remaining unoccupied", or as a measure to prevent the pharaoh's riches from falling into the hands of his rivals or successors. Pliny does not speculate as to the pharaoh in question, explicitly noting that "accident consigned to oblivion the names of those who erected such stupendous memorials of their vanity". In pondering how the stones could be transported to such a vast height he gives two explanations: That either vast mounds of nitre and salt were heaped up against the pyramid which were then melted away with water redirected from the river. Or, that "bridges" were constructed, their bricks afterwards distributed for erecting houses of private individuals, arguing that the level of the river is too low for canals to ever bring water up to the pyramid. Pliny also recounts how "in the interior of the largest Pyramid there is a well, eighty-six cubits [45.1 m; 147.8 ft] deep, which communicates with the river, it is thought". Further, he describes a method discovered by Thales of Miletus for ascertaining the pyramid's height by measuring its shadow.

- Further information: Joseph's Granaries

During late antiquity, a misinterpretation of the pyramids as "Joseph's granary" began to gain in popularity. The first textual evidence of this connection is found in the travel narratives of the female Christian pilgrim Egeria, who records that on her visit between 381–384 AD, "in the twelve-mile stretch between Memphis and Babylonia [= Old Cairo] are many pyramids, which Joseph made in order to store corn."Ten years later the usage is confirmed in the anonymous travelogue of seven monks that set out from Jerusalem to visit the famous ascetics in Egypt, wherein they report that they "saw Joseph's granaries, where he stored grain in biblical times." This late 4th century usage is further confirmed in the geographical treatise Cosmographia, written by Julius Honorius around 376 AD, which explains that the Pyramids were called the "granaries of Joseph" (horrea Ioseph). This reference from Julius is important, as it indicates that the identification was starting to spread out from pilgrim's travelogues. In 530 AD, Stephanos of Byzantium added more to this idea when he wrote in his Ethnica that the word "pyramid" was connected to the Greek word πυρός (puros), meaning wheat.

- The Abbasid Caliph Al-Ma'mun (786–833 AD) is said to have tunneled into the side of the Great Pyramid

In the seventh century AD, the Rashidun Caliphate conquered Egypt, ending several centuries of Romano-Byzantine rule. A few centuries later, in

820 AD, the Abbasid Caliph Al-Ma'mun (786–833) is said to have tunneled into the side of the structure and discovered the ascending passage and its connecting chambers. Around this time a Coptic legend gained popularity that claimed the antediluvian king Surid Ibn Salhouk had built the Pyramid. One legend in particular relates how, three hundred years prior to the Great Flood, Surid had a terrifying dream of the world's end, and so he ordered the construction of the pyramids so that they might house all the knowledge of Egypt and survive into the present. The most notable account of this legend was given by Al-Masudi (896–956) in his Akbar al-zaman, alongside imaginative tales about the pyramid, such as the story of a man who fell three hours down the pyramid's well and the tale of an expedition that discovered bizarre finds in the structure's inner chambers. Al-zaman also contains a report of Al-Ma'mun's entering the pyramid and discovering a vessel containing a thousand coins, which just so happened to account for the cost of opening the pyramid. (Some speculate that this story is true, but that the coins were planted by Al-Ma'mun to appease his workers, who were likely frustrated that they had found no treasure.)

In 987 AD, the Arab bibliographer Ibn al-Nadim relates a fantastical tale in his Al-Fihrist about a man who journeyed into the main chamber of a pyramid, which Bayard Dodge argues is the Great Pyramid. According to al-Nadim, the person in question saw a statue of a man holding a tablet and a woman holding a mirror. Supposedly, between the statues was a "stone vessel a gold cover." Inside the vessel was "something like pitch," and when the explorer reached into the vessel "a gold receptacle happened to be inside." The receptacle, when taken from the vessel, was filled with "fresh blood," which quickly dried up. Ibn al-Nadim's work also claims that the bodies of a man and woman were discovered inside the Pyramid in the "best possible state of preservation.

" The author al-Kaisi, in his work the Tohfat Alalbab, retells the story of Al-Ma'mun's entry but with the additional discovery of "an image of a man in green stone", which when opened revealed a body dressed in jewel-encrusted gold armor. Al-Kaisi claims to have seen the case from which the body was taken, and asserts that it was located at the king's palace in Cairo. He also writes that he himself entered into the pyramid and discovered myriad preserved bodies.

The Arab polymath Abd al-Latif al-Baghdadi (1163–1231) studied the pyramid with great care, and in his Account of Egypt, he praises them as works of engineering genius. In addition to measuring the structure (alongside the other pyramids at Giza), al-Baghdadi also writes that the structures were surely tombs, although he thought the Great Pyramid was used for the burial of Agathodaimon or Hermes. Al-Baghdadi ponders whether the pyramid pre-dated the Great flood as described in Genesis, and even briefly entertained the idea that it was a pre-Adamic construction. A few centuries later, the Islamic historian Al-Maqrizi (1364–1442) compiled lore about the Great Pyramid in his Al-Khitat. In addition to reasserting that Al-Ma'mun breached the structure in 820 AD, Al-Maqrizi's work also discusses the sarcophagus in the coffin chambers, explicitly noting that the pyramid was a grave.

By the close of the Middle Ages, the Great Pyramid had gained a reputation as a haunted structure. Others feared entering because it was home to animals like bats.

- Construction Preparation of the site

A hillock forms the base on which the pyramids stands. It was cut back into steps and only a strip around the perimeter was leveled, which has been measured to be horizontal and flat to within 21 millimetres (0.8 in). The bedrock reaches a height of almost 6 metres (20 ft) above the pyramid base at the location of the Grotto.

Along the sides of the base platform a series of holes are cut in the bedrock. Lehner hypothesizes that they held wooden posts used for alignment. Edwards, among others, suggested the usage of water for evening the base, although it is unclear how practical and workable such a system would be.

- Materials

The Great Pyramid consists of an estimated 2.3 million blocks. Approximately 5.5 million tonnes of limestone, 8,000 tonnes of granite, and 500,000 tonnes of mortar were used in the construction.

Most of the blocks were quarried at Giza just south of the pyramid, an area now known as the Central Field.

The white limestone used for the casing originated from Tura (10 km (6.2 mi) south of Giza) and was transported by boat down the Nile. In 2013, rolls of papyrus called the Diary of Merer were discovered, written by a supervisor of the deliveries of limestone and other construction materials from Tura to Giza in the last known year of Khufu's reign.

The granite stones in the pyramid were transported from Aswan, more than 900 km (560 mi) away. The largest, weighing 25 to 80 tonnes, form the roofs of the "King's chamber" and the "relieving chambers" above it. Ancient Egyptians cut stone into rough blocks by hammering grooves into natural stone faces, inserting wooden wedges, then soaking these with water. As the water was absorbed, the wedges expanded, breaking off workable chunks. Once the blocks were cut, they were carried by boat either up or down the Nile River to the pyramid.

- Workforce

The Greeks believed that slave labour was used, but modern discoveries made at nearby workers' camps associated with construction at Giza suggest that it was built instead by thousands of conscript laborers.

Worker graffiti found at Giza suggest haulers were divided into zau (singular za), groups of 40 men, consisting of four sub-units that each had an "Overseer of Ten".

As to the question of how over two million blocks could have been cut within Khufu's lifetime, stonemason Franck Burgos conducted an archaeological experiment based on an abandoned quarry of Khufu discovered in 2017. Within it, an almost completed block and the tools used for cutting it had been uncovered: Hardened arsenic copper chisels, wooden mallets, ropes and stone tools. In the experiment replicas of these were used to cut a block weighing about 2.5 tonnes (the average block size used for the Great Pyramid). It took 4 workers 4 days (with each working 6 hours a day) to excavate it. The initially slow progress sped up six times when the stone was wetted with water. Based on the data, Burgos extrapolates that about 3,500 quarry-men could have produced the 250 blocks/day needed to complete the Great Pyramid in 27 years.

A construction management study conducted in 1999, in association with Mark Lehner and other Egyptologists, had estimated that the total project required an average workforce of about 13,200 people and a peak workforce of roughly 40,000.

- Surveys

Comparison of approximate profiles of the Great Pyramid of Giza with some notable pyramidal or near-pyramidal buildings. Dotted lines indicate original heights, where data is available. In its SVG file, hover over a pyramid to highlight and click for its article.

- The first precise measurements of the pyramid were made by Egyptologist Flinders Petrie in 1880–1882, published as The Pyramids and Temples of Gizeh. Many of the casing-stones and inner chamber blocks of the Great Pyramid fit together with high precision, with joints, on average, only 0.5 millimetres (0.020 in) wide.On the contrary, core blocks were only roughly shaped, with rubble inserted between larger gaps. Mortar was used to bind the outer layers together and fill gaps and joints.

The block height and weight tends to get progressively smaller towards the top. Petrie measured the lowest layer to be 148 centimetres (4.86 ft) high, whereas the layers towards the summit barely exceed 50 centimetres (1.6 ft).

- The accuracy of the pyramid's perimeter is such that the four sides of the base have an average error of only 58 millimetres (2.3 inches) in length and the finished base was squared to a mean corner error of only 12 seconds of arc.

The completed design dimensions are measured to have originally been 280 royal cubits (146.7 m; 481.4 ft) high by 440 cubits (230.6 m; 756.4 ft) long at each of the four sides of its base. Ancient Egyptians used Seked - how much run for one cubit of rise - to describe slopes. For the Great Pyramid a Seked of 5+1/2 palms was chosen; a ratio of 14 up to 11 in.

Some Egyptologists suggest this slope was chosen because the ratio of perimeter to height (1760/280 cubits) equates to 2π to an accuracy of better than 0.05 percent (corresponding to the well-known approximation of π as 22/7). Verner wrote, "We can conclude that although the ancient Egyptians could not precisely define the value of π, in practice they used it". Petrie concluded: "but these relations of areas and of circular ratio are so systematic that we should grant that they were in the builder's design". Others have argued that the ancient Egyptians had no concept of pi and would not have thought to encode it in their monuments and that the observed pyramid slope may be based on the seked choice alone.

- Alignment to the cardinal directions

The sides of the Great Pyramid's base are closely aligned to the four geographic (not magnetic) cardinal directions, deviating on average 3 minutes and 38 seconds of arc. Several methods have been proposed for how the ancient Egyptians achieved this level of accuracy:

The Solar Gnomon Method - The shadow of a vertical rod is tracked throughout a day. The shadow line is intersected by a circle drawn around the base of the rod. Connecting the intersecting points produces an east-west line. An experiment using this method resulted in lines being, on average, 2 minutes, 9 seconds off due east-west. Employing a pinhole produced much more accurate results (19 arc seconds off), whereas using an angled block as a shadow definer was less accurate (3'47" off).

The Pole Star Method - The polar star is tracked using a movable sight and fixed plumb line. Halfway between the maximum eastern and western elongations is true north. Thuban, the polar star during the Old Kingdom, was about two degrees removed from the celestial pole at the time.

The Simultaneous Transit Method - The stars Mizar and Kochab appear on a vertical line on the horizon, close to true north around 2500 BC. They slowly and simultaneously shift east over time, which is used to explain the relative misalignment of the pyramids.

- Egyptian pyramid construction techniques

Many alternative, often contradictory, theories have been proposed regarding the pyramid's construction techniques. One mystery of the pyramid's construction is its planning. John Romer suggests that they used the same method that had been used for earlier and later constructions, laying out parts of the plan on the ground at a 1-to-1 scale. He writes that "such a working diagram would also serve to generate the architecture of the pyramid with precision unmatched by any other means".

The basalt blocks of the pyramid temple show "clear evidence" of having been cut with some kind of saw with an estimated cutting blade of 15 feet (4.6 m) in length. Romer suggests that this "super saw" may have had copper teeth and weighed up to 140 kilograms (310 lb). He theorizes that such a saw could have been attached to a wooden trestle support and possibly used in conjunction with vegetable oil, cutting sand, emery or pounded quartz to cut the blocks, which would have required the labour of at least a dozen men to operate it.

- Casing stone in the British Museum

At completion, the Great Pyramid was cased entirely in white limestone. Precisely worked blocks were placed in horizontal layers and carefully fitted together with mortar, their outward faces cut at a slope and smoothed to a high degree. Together they created four uniform surfaces. Unfinished casing blocks of the pyramids of Menkaure and Henutsen at Giza suggest that the front faces were smoothed only after the stones were laid, with chiseled seams marking correct positioning and where the superfluous rock would have to be trimmed off.

The height of the horizontal layers is not uniform but varies considerably. The highest of the 203 remaining courses are towards the bottom, the first layer being the tallest at 1.49 metres (4.9 ft). Towards the top, layers tend to be only slightly over 1 royal cubit (0.5 m; 1.7 ft) in height. An irregular pattern is noticeable when looking at the sizes in sequence, where layer height declines steadily only to rise sharply again.

So-called "backing stones" supported the casing which were (unlike core blocks) precisely dressed as well and bound to the casing with mortar. Nowadays, these stones give the structure its visible appearance, following the dismantling of the pyramid in the middle ages. In 1303 AD, a massive earthquake had loosened many of the outer casing stones, which were said to have been carted away by Bahri Sultan An-Nasir Nasir-ad-Din al-Hasan in 1356 for use in nearby Cairo. Many more casing stones were removed from the site by Muhammad Ali Pasha in the early 19th century to build the upper portion of his Alabaster Mosque in Cairo, not far from Giza.

Later explorers reported massive piles of rubble at the base of the pyramids left over from the continuing collapse of the casing stones, which were subsequently cleared away during continuing excavations of the site. Today a few of the casing stones from the lowest course can be seen in situ on each side, with the best preserved on the north below the entrances, excavated by Vyse in 1837.

The mortar was chemically analyzed and contains organic inclusions (mostly coal), samples of which were radiocarbon dated to 2871–2604 BC. It has been theorized that the mortar enabled the masons to set the stones exactly by providing a level bed.

It has been suggested that some or all of the casing stones were cast in place, rather than quarried and moved, yet archaeological evidence and petrographic analysis indicate this was not the case.

Petrie noted in 1880 that the sides of the pyramid, as we see them today, are "very distinctly hollowed" and that "each side has a sort of groove specially down the middle of the face", which he reasoned was a result of increased casing thickness in these areas.A laser scanning survey in 2005 confirmed the existence of the anomalies, which can be, to some degree, attributed to damaged and removed stones. Under certain lighting conditions and with image enhancement the faces can appear to be split, leading to speculation that the pyramid had been intentionally constructed eight-sided.

- Pyramidion and missing tip

The pyramid was once topped by a capstone known as a pyramidion. The material it was made from is subject to much speculation; limestone, granite or basalt are commonly proposed, while in popular culture it is often solid gold or gilded. All known 4th dynasty pyramidia (of the Red Pyramid, Satellite Pyramid of Khufu (G1-d) and Queen's Pyramid of Menkaure (G3-a)) are of white limestone and were not gilded. Only from the 5th dynasty onward is there evidence of gilded capstones; for instance, a scene on the causeway of the Sahure speaks of the "white gold pyramidion of the pyramid Sahure's Soul Shines".

The Great Pyramid's pyramidion was already lost in antiquity, as Pliny the Elder and later authors report of a platform on its summit. Nowadays the pyramid is about 8 metres (26 ft) shorter than it was when intact, with about 1,000 tonnes of material missing from the top.

In 1874 a mast was installed on the top by the Scottish astronomer Sir David Gill who, whilst returning from work involving observing a rare Venus transit, was invited to survey Egypt and began by surveying the Great Pyramid. His results measuring the pyramid were accurate to within 1mm and the survey mast is still in place to this day.

- Original entrance

The original entrance is located on the north side, 15 royal cubits (7.9 m; 25.8 ft) east of the centerline of the pyramid. Before the removal of the casing in the middle ages, the pyramid was entered through a hole in the 19th layer of masonry, approximately 17 metres (56 ft) above the pyramid's base level. The height of that layer – 96 centimetres (3.15 ft) – corresponds to the size of the entrance tunnel which is commonly called the Descending Passage. According to Strabo (64–24 BC) a movable stone could be raised to enter this sloping corridor, however it is not known if it was a later addition or original.

A row of double chevrons diverts weight away from the entrance. Several of these chevron blocks are now missing, as the slanted faces they used to rest on indicate.

Numerous, mostly modern, graffiti is cut into the stones around the entrance. Most notable is a large, square text of hieroglyphs carved in honor of Frederick William IV, by Karl Richard Lepsius's Prussian expedition to Egypt in 1842.

- North Face Corridor

In 2016 the ScanPyramids team detected a cavity behind the entrance chevrons using muography, which was confirmed in 2019 to be a corridor at least 5 metres (16 ft) long, running horizontal or sloping upwards (thus not parallel to the Descending Passage). Whether or not it connects to the Big Void above the Grand Gallery remains to be seen.

- Robbers' Tunnel

Today tourists enter the Great Pyramid via the Robbers‘ Tunnel, which was long ago cut straight through the masonry of the pyramid. The entrance was forced into the 6th and 7th layer of the casing, about 7 metres (23 ft) above the base. After running more-or-less straight and horizontal for 27 metres (89 ft) it turns sharply left to encounter the blocking stones in the Ascending Passage. It is possible to enter the Descending Passage from this point but access is usually forbidden.

The origin of this Robbers' Tunnel is the subject of much scholarly discussion. According to tradition the chasm was made around 820 AD by Caliph al-Ma‘mun's workmen with a battering ram. The digging dislodged the stone in the ceiling of the Descending Passage which hid the entrance to the Ascending Passage, and the noise of that stone falling then sliding down the Descending Passage alerted them to the need to turn left. Unable to remove these stones, however, the workmen tunneled up beside them through the softer limestone of the Pyramid until they reached the Ascending Passage.

Due to a number of historical and archaeological discrepancies, many scholars (with Antoine de Sacy perhaps being the first) contend that this story is apocryphal. They argue that it is much more likely that the tunnel had been carved sometime after the pyramid was initially sealed. This tunnel, the scholars continue, was then resealed (likely during the Ramesside Restoration), and it was this plug that al-Ma'mun's ninth-century expedition cleared away. This theory is furthered by the report of patriarch Dionysius I Telmaharoyo, who claimed that before al-Ma'mun's expedition, there already existed a breach in the pyramid's north face that extended into the structure 33 metres (108 ft) before hitting a dead end. This suggests that some sort of robber's tunnel predated al-Ma'mun, and that the caliph simply enlarged it and cleared it of debris.

- Descending Passage

From the original entrance, a passage descends through the masonry of the pyramid and then into the bedrock beneath it, ultimately leading to the Subterranean Chamber.

It has a slanted height of 4 Egyptian feet (1.20 m; 3.9 ft) and a width of 2 cubits (1.0 m; 3.4 ft). Its angle of 26°26'46" corresponds to a ratio of 1 to 2 (rise over run).

After 28 metres (92 ft), the lower end of the Ascending Passage is reached; a square hole in the ceiling, which is blocked by granite stones and might have originally been concealed. To circumvent these hard stones, a short tunnel was excavated that meets the end of the Robbers' Tunnel. This was expanded over time and fitted with stairs.

The passage continues to descend for another 72 metres (236 ft), now through bedrock instead of the pyramid superstructure. Lazy guides used to block off this part with rubble to avoid having to lead people down and back up the long shaft, until around 1902 when Covington installed a padlocked iron grill-door to stop this practice.Near the end of this section, on the west wall, is the connection to the vertical shaft that leads up to the Grand Gallery.

A horizontal shaft connects the end of the Descending Passage to the Subterranean Chamber, It has a length of 8.84 m (29.0 ft), width of 85 cm (2.79 ft) and height of 91–95 cm (2.99–3.12 ft). A recess is located towards the end of the western wall, slightly larger than the tunnel, the ceiling of which is irregular and undressed.

- Subterranean Chamber

Subterranean Chamber (looking west) in 1909 with rubble from the Pit Shaft excavation still filling the chamber.Subterranean Chamber (looking south) with Pit Shaft in the floor and blind corridor entrance.The Subterranean Chamber, or simply "Pit", is the lowest of the three main chambers and the only one dug into the bedrock beneath the pyramid.It is rectangular and measures roughly 16 cubits (8.4 m; 27.5 ft) north-south by 27 cubits (14.1 m; 46.4 ft) east-west, with an approximate height of 4 m (13 ft). It is located about 27 m (89 ft) below base level.

The western half of the room, apart from the ceiling, is clearly unfinished, with trenches left behind by the quarry-men running east to west. A niche was cut into the northern half of the west wall. The only access, through the Descending Passage, lies on the eastern end of the north wall.

Although seemingly known in antiquity, according to Herodotus and later authors, its existence had been forgotten in the middle ages. It was rediscovered only in 1817 by Giovanni Battista Caviglia, after he cleared the rubble blocking the Descending Passage.

Opposite the entrance, a blind corridor runs straight south for 11 m (36 ft) and continues slight bent another 5.4 m (18 ft), measuring about 0.75 m (2.5 ft) squared. A Greek or Roman character was found on its ceiling with the light of a candle, suggesting that the chamber had indeed been accessible during ancient Roman times.

In the middle of the eastern half, a large hole is opened up, usually called Pit Shaft or Perring's Shaft. The upmost part seems to have ancient origins, about 2 m (6.6 ft) squared in width and 1.5 m (4.9 ft) in depth, diagonally aligned with the chamber. Caviglia and Salt enlarged it to the depth of about 3 m (9.8 ft).

In 1837 Vyse directed the shaft to be sunk to a depth of 50 ft (15 m), in hopes of discovering the chamber encompassed by water that Herodotus alludes to. It was made slightly narrower, about 1.5 m (4.9 ft) in width, hence is easy to be distinguished. But no chamber was discovered after Perring and his workers had spent one and a half years penetrating the bedrock to the then water level of the Nile, some 12 m (39 ft) further down.

The rubble produced during this operation was deposited throughout the chamber. When Petrie visited the pyramid in 1880 he found the shaft to be partially filled with water that had rushed down the Descending Passage during heavy rainfalls. In 1909, when the Edgar brothers‘ surveying activities were encumbered by the material, they moved the sand and smaller stones back into the shaft, leaving the upper part of it clear. The deep, modern shaft is sometimes mistaken to be part of the original design.

Some Egyptologists suggest that this Lower Chamber was intended to be the original burial chamber, but that Pharaoh Khufu later changed his mind and wanted it to be higher up in the pyramid.

1. The upper two granite plugs in the Ascending Passage, seen from the end of the Robbers' Tunnel.

The Ascending Passage connects the Descending Passage to the Grand Gallery. It is 75 cubits (39.3 m; 128.9 ft) long and of the same width and height as the shaft it originates from, although its angle is slightly lower at 26°6‘.

The lower end of the shaft is plugged by three granite stones, which were slid down from the Grand Gallery to seal the tunnel. They are 1.57 m (5.2 ft), 1.67 m (5.5 ft) and 1 m (3.3 ft) long respectively. The uppermost is heavily damaged, hence it is shorter. The end of the Robbers' Tunnel concludes slightly below the stones, so a short tunnel was dug around them to gain access to the Descending Passage, since the surrounding limestone is considerably softer and easier to work.

Most of the joints between the blocks of the walls run perpendicular to the floor, with two exceptions. Firstly, those in the lower third of the corridor are vertical. Secondly, the three girdle stones that are inserted near the middle (about 10 cubits apart), presumably to stabilize the tunnel.

- Well Shaft and Grotto

The Well Shaft (also known as the Service Shaft or Vertical Shaft) links the lower end of the Grand Gallery to the bottom of Descending Passage, about 50 metres (160 ft) further down.

It takes a winding and indirect course. The upper half goes through the nucleus masonry of the pyramid. It runs vertical at first for 8 metres (26 ft), then slightly angled southwards for about the same distance, until it hits bedrock approximately 5.7 metres (19 ft) above the pyramid's base level. Another vertical section descends further, which is partially lined with masonry that has been broken through to a cavity known as the Grotto. The lower half of the Well Shaft goes through the bedrock at an angle of about 45° for 26.5 metres (87 ft) before a steeper section, 9.5 metres (31 ft) long, leads to its lowest point. The final section of 2.6 metres (8.5 ft) connects it to the Descending Passage, running almost horizontal. The builders evidently had trouble aligning the lower exit.

The purpose of the shaft is commonly explained as a ventilation shaft for the Subterranean Chamber and as an escape shaft for the workers who slid the blocking stones of the Ascending Passage into place.

The Grotto is a natural limestone cave that was likely filled with sand and gravel before construction, before being hollowed out by looters. A granite block rests in it that likely originated from the portcullis that once sealed the King's Chamber.

- Axonometric view of the Queen's Chamber

The Horizontal Passage links the Grand Gallery to the Queen's Chamber. Five pairs of holes at the start suggest the tunnel was once concealed with slabs that laid flush with the gallery floor. The passage is 2 cubits (1.0 m; 3.4 ft) wide and 1.17 m (3.8 ft) high for most of its length, but near the chamber there is a step in the floor, after which the passage increases to 1.68 m (5.5 ft) high.Half of the west-wall consists of two layers that have atypically continuous vertical joints. Dormion suggests the entrances to magazines laid here and have been filled in.

The "Queen's Chamber" is exactly halfway between the north and south faces of the pyramid. It measures 10 cubits (5.2 m; 17.2 ft) north-south, 11 cubits (5.8 m; 18.9 ft) east-west,and has a pointed roof that apexes at 12 cubits (6.3 m; 20.6 ft) tall. At the eastern end of the chamber there is a niche 9 cubits (4.7 m; 15.5 ft) high. The original depth of the niche was 2 cubits (1.0 m; 3.4 ft), but it has since been deepened by treasure hunters.

Shafts were discovered in the north and south walls of the Queen's Chamber in 1872 by British engineer Waynman Dixon, who believed shafts similar to those in the King's Chamber must also exist. The shafts were not connected to the outer faces of the pyramid or the Queen's Chamber; their purpose is unknown. In one shaft Dixon discovered a ball of diorite, a bronze hook of unknown purpose and a piece of cedar wood. The first two objects are currently in the British Museum. The latter was lost until recently when it was found at the University of Aberdeen It has since been radiocarbon dated to 3341–3094 BC. The northern shaft's angle of ascent fluctuates and at one point turns 45 degrees to avoid the Great Gallery. The southern shaft is perpendicular to the pyramid's slope.

The shafts in the Queen's Chamber were explored in 1993 by the German engineer Rudolf Gantenbrink using a crawler robot he designed, Upuaut 2. After a climb of 65 m (213 ft), he discovered that one of the shafts was blocked by a limestone "door" with two eroded copper "handles". The National Geographic Society created a similar robot which, in September 2002, drilled a small hole in the southern door only to find another stone slab behind it. The northern passage, which was difficult to navigate because of its twists and turns, was also found to be blocked by a slab.

Research continued in 2011 with the Djedi Project which used a fibre-optic "micro snake camera" that could see around corners. With this, they were able to penetrate the first door of the southern shaft through the hole drilled in 2002, and view all the sides of the small chamber behind it. They discovered hieroglyphics written in red paint. Egyptian mathematics researcher Luca Miatello stated that the markings read "121" – the length of the shaft in cubits. The Djedi team were also able to scrutinize the inside of the two copper "handles" embedded in the door, which they now believe to be for decorative purposes. They additionally found the reverse side of the "door" to be finished and polished, which suggests that it was not put there just to block the shaft from debris, but rather for a more specific reason.

- Grand Gallery

The Grand Gallery continues the slope of the Ascending Passage towards the King's Chamber, extending from the 23rd to the 48th course, a rise of 21 metres (69 ft). It has been praised as a "truly spectacular example of stonemasonry". It is 8.6 metres (28 ft) high and 46.68 metres (153.1 ft) long. The base is 4 cubits (2.1 m; 6.9 ft) wide, but after two courses – at a height of 2.29 metres (7.5 ft) – the blocks of stone in the walls are corbelled inwards by 6–10 centimetres (2.4–3.9 in) on each side. There are seven of these steps, so, at the top, the Grand Gallery is only 2 cubits (1.0 m; 3.4 ft) wide. It is roofed by slabs of stone laid at a slightly steeper angle than the floor so that each stone fits into a slot cut into the top of the gallery, like the teeth of a ratchet. The purpose was to have each block supported by the wall of the Gallery, rather than resting on the block beneath it, in order to prevent cumulative pressure.

At the upper end of the Gallery, on the eastern wall, there is a hole near the roof that opens into a short tunnel by which access can be gained to the lowest of the Relieving Chambers.

The floor of the Grand Gallery has a shelf or step on either side, 1 cubit (52.4 cm; 20.6 in) wide, leaving a lower ramp 2 cubits (1.0 m; 3.4 ft) wide between them. There are 56 slots on the shelves, with 28 on each side. On each wall, 25 niches have been cut above the slots. The purpose of these slots is not known, but the central gutter in the floor of the Gallery, which is the same width as the Ascending Passage, has led to speculation that the blocking stones were stored in the Grand Gallery and the slots held wooden beams to restrain them from sliding down the passage. Jean-Pierre Houdin theorized that they held a timber frame that was used in combination with a trolley to pull the heavy granite blocks up the pyramid.

At the top of the gallery, there is a step onto a small horizontal platform where a tunnel leads through the Antechamber, once blocked by portcullis stones, into the King's Chamber.

- The Big Void

In 2017, scientists from the ScanPyramids project discovered a large cavity above the Grand Gallery using muon radiography, which they called the "ScanPyramids Big Void". Key was a research team under Professor Morishima Kunihiro from Nagoya University that used special nuclear emulsion detectors.[Its length is at least 30 metres (98 ft) and its cross-section is similar to that of the Grand Gallery. Its existence was confirmed by independent detection with three different technologies: nuclear emulsion films, scintillator hodoscopes, and gas detectors.The purpose of the cavity is unknown and it is not accessible. Zahi Hawass speculates it may have been a gap used in the construction of the Grand Gallery, but the Japanese research team state that the void is completely different from previously identified construction spaces.

To verify and pinpoint the void, a team from Kyushu University, Tohoku University, the University of Tokyo and the Chiba Institute of Technology planned to rescan the structure with a newly developed muon detector in 2020. Their work was delayed by the COVID-19 pandemic.

- Antechamber

The last line of defense against intrusion was a small chamber specially designed to house portcullis blocking stones, called the Antechamber. It is cased almost entirely in granite and is situated between the upper end of the Grand Gallery and the King's Chamber. Three slots for portcullis stones line the east and west wall of the chamber. Each of them is topped with a semi-circular groove for a log, around which ropes could be spanned.

The granite portcullis stones were approximately 1 cubit (52.4 cm; 20.6 in) thick and were lowered into position by the aforementioned ropes which were tied through a series of four holes at the top of the blocks. A corresponding set of four vertical grooves are on the south wall of the chamber, recesses that make space for the ropes.

The Antechamber has a design flaw: the space above them can be accessed, thus all but the last block can be circumvented. This was exploited by looters who punched a hole through the ceiling of the tunnel behind, gaining access to the King's Chamber. Later on, all three portcullis stones were broken and removed. Fragments of these blocks can be found in various locations in the pyramid.

- Axonometric view of the King's Chamber

The King's Chamber is the upmost of the three main chambers of the pyramid. It is faced entirely with granite and measures 20 cubits (10.5 m; 34.4 ft) east-west by 10 cubits (5.2 m; 17.2 ft) north-south. Its flat ceiling is about 11 cubits and 5 digits (5.8 m;19.0 ft) above the floor, formed by nine slabs of stone weighing in total about 400 tons. All the roof beams show cracks due to the chamber having settled 2.5–5 cm (0.98–1.97 in).

The walls consist of five courses of blocks that are uninscribed, as was the norm for burial chambers of the 4th dynasty. The stones are precisely fitted together. The facing surfaces are dressed to varying degrees, with some displaying remains of bosses not entirely cut away. The back sides of the blocks were only roughly hewn to shape, as was usual with Egyptian hard-stone facade blocks, presumably to save work.

- Sarcophagus in the King's Chamber

The only object in the King's Chamber is a sarcophagus made out of a single, hollowed-out granite block. When it was rediscovered in the early middle ages, it was found broken open and any contents had already been removed. It is of the form common for early Egyptian sarcophagi; rectangular in shape with grooves to slide the now missing lid into place with three small holes for pegs to fixate it. The coffer was not perfectly smoothed, displaying various tool marks matching those of copper saws and tubular hand-drills.

The internal dimensions are roughly 198 cm (6.50 ft) by 68 cm (2.23 feet), the external 228 cm (7.48 ft) by 98 cm (3.22 ft), with a height of 105 cm (3.44 ft). The walls have a thickness of about 15 cm (0.49 ft). The sarcophagus is too large to fit around the corner between the Ascending and Descending Passages, which indicates that it must have been placed in the chamber before the roof was put in place.

- Air shafts

In the north and south walls of the King's Chamber are two narrow shafts, commonly known as "air shafts". They face each other and are located approximately 0.91 m (3.0 ft) above the floor, 2.5 m (8.2 ft) from the eastern wall, with a width of 18 and 21 cm (7.1 and 8.3 in) and a height of 14 cm (5.5 in). Both start out horizontally for the length of the granite blocks they go through before changing to an upwards direction. The southern shaft ascends at an angle of 45° with a slight curve westwards. One ceiling stone was found to be distinctly unfinished which Gantenbrink called a "Monday morning block". The northern shaft changes angle several times, shifting the path to the west, perhaps to avoid the Big Void. The builders had trouble calculating the right angles, resulting in parts of the shaft being narrower. Nowadays they both commute to the exterior. If they originally penetrated the outer casing is unknown.

The purpose of these shafts is not clear: They were long believed by Egyptologists to be shafts for ventilation, but this idea has now been widely abandoned in favour of the shafts serving a ritualistic purpose associated with the ascension of the king's spirit to the heavens. Ironically, both shafts were fitted with ventilators in 1992 to reduce the humidity in the pyramid.

The idea that the shafts point towards stars or areas of the northern and southern skies has been largely dismissed as the northern shaft follows a dog-leg course through the masonry and the southern shaft has a bend of approximately 20 centimetres (7.9 in), indicating no intention to have them point to any celestial objects.

- Relieving Chambers above the King's Chamber, Smyth 1877

Above the roof of the King's Chamber are five compartments, named (from lowest upwards) "Davison's Chamber", "Wellington's Chamber", "Nelson's Chamber", "Lady Arbuthnot's Chamber", and "Campbell's Chamber".

They were presumably intended to safeguard the King's Chamber from the possibility of the roof collapsing under the weight of stone above, hence they are referred to as "Relieving Chambers".

The granite blocks that divide the chambers have flat bottom sides but roughly shaped top sides, giving all five chambers an irregular floor, but a flat ceiling, with the exception of the uppermost chamber which has a pointed limestone roof.

Nathaniel Davison is credited with the discovery of the lowest of these chambers in 1763, although a French merchant named Maynard informed him of its existence.It can be reached through an ancient passage that originates from the top of the south wall of the Grand Gallery.The upper four chambers were discovered in 1837 by Howard Vyse after a crack in the ceiling of the first chamber. This allowed the insertion of a long reed, which, with the employment of gunpowder and boring rods, forced a tunnel upwards through the masonry. As no access shafts existed for the upper four chambers – unlike Davison's Chamber – they were completely inaccessible until this point.

Numerous graffiti of red ochre paint were found to cover the limestone walls of all four newly discovered chambers. Apart from leveling lines and indication marks for masons, multiple hieroglyphic inscriptions spell out the names of work-gangs. Those names, which were also found in other Egyptian pyramids like that of Menkaure and Sahure, usually included the name of the pharaoh they were working for. The blocks must have received the inscriptions before the chambers became inaccessible during construction. Their orientation, often side-ways or upside down, and their sometimes being partially covered by blocks, seems to indicate that the stones were inscribed before being laid.

- Remains of the basalt floor of the temple at the east foot of the pyramid

The Pyramid Temple, which stood on the east side of the pyramid and measured 52.2 metres (171 ft) north to south and 40 metres (130 ft) east to west, has almost entirely disappeared. Only some of the black basalt paving has remained. There are only a few remnants of the causeway which linked the pyramid with the valley and the Valley Temple. The Valley Temple is buried beneath the village of Nazlet el-Samman; basalt paving and limestone walls have been found but the site has not been excavated.

- East cemetery

The tomb of Queen Hetepheres I, sister-wife of Sneferu and mother of Khufu, is located approximately 110 metres (360 ft) east of the Great Pyramid. Discovered by accident by the Reisner expedition, the burial was intact, although the carefully sealed coffin proved to be empty.

- Subsidiary pyramids

On the southern end of the east side are four subsidiary pyramids The three that remain standing to almost full height are popularly known as the Queens‘ Pyramids (G1-a, G1-b and G1-c). The fourth, smaller satellite pyramid (G1-d), was so ruined that its existence was not suspected until the first course of stones and, later, the remains of the capstone were discovered during excavations in 1991–93.

- Khufu ship and Solar barque

Three boat-shaped pits are located east of the pyramid. They are large enough in size and shape to have held complete boats, though so shallow that any superstructure, if there ever was one, must have been removed or disassembled.

Two additional boat pits, long and rectangular in shape, were found south of the pyramid, still covered with slabs of stone weighing up to 15 tons.

The first of these was discovered in May 1954 by the Egyptian archaeologist Kamal el-Mallakh. Inside were 1,224 pieces of wood, the longest 23 metres (75 ft) in length, the shortest 10 centimetres (0.33 ft). These were entrusted to a boat builder, Haj Ahmed Yusuf, who worked out how the pieces fit together. The entire process, including conservation and straightening of the warped wood, took fourteen years. The result is a cedar-wood boat 43.6 metres (143 ft) long, its timbers held together by ropes, which was originally housed in the Giza Solar boat museum, a special boat-shaped, air-conditioned museum beside the pyramid. It is now in the Grand Egyptian Museum.

During construction of this museum in the 1980s, the second sealed boat pit was discovered. It was left unopened until 2011 when excavation began on the boat.

- Pyramid town

A notable construction flanking the Giza pyramid complex is a cyclopean stone wall, the Wall of the Crow. Mark Lehner discovered a worker's town outside of the wall, otherwise known as "The Lost City", dated by pottery styles, seal impressions and stratigraphy to have been constructed and occupied sometime during the reigns of Khafre (2520–2494 BC) and Menkaure (2490–2472 BC). In the early 21st century, Lehner and his team made several discoveries, including what appears to have been a thriving port, suggesting the town and associated living quarters, which consisted of barracks called "galleries", may not have been for the pyramid workers after all, but rather for the soldiers and sailors who utilized the port. In light of this new discovery, as to where then the pyramid workers may have lived, Lehner suggested the alternative possibility they may have camped on the ramps he believes were used to construct the pyramids, or possibly at nearby quarries.

In the early 1970s, the Australian archaeologist Karl Kromer excavated a mound in the South Field of the plateau. It was found to contain artefacts including mudbrick seals of Khufu, which he identified with an artisans' settlement. Mudbrick buildings just south of Khufu's Valley Temple contained mud sealings of Khufu and have been suggested to be a settlement serving the cult of Khufu after his death. A worker's cemetery used at least between Khufu's reign and the end of the Fifth Dynasty was discovered south of the Wall of the Crow by Hawass in 1990.

- Looting

Authors Bob Brier and Hoyt Hobbs claim that "all the pyramids were robbed" by the New Kingdom, when the construction of royal tombs in the Valley of the Kings began. Joyce Tyldesley states that the Great Pyramid itself "is known to have been opened and emptied by the Middle Kingdom", before the Arab caliph Al-Ma‘mun entered the pyramid around 820 AD.

I. E. S. Edwards discusses Strabo's mention that the pyramid "a little way up one side has a stone that may be taken out, which being raised up there is a sloping passage to the foundations". Edwards suggested that the pyramid was entered by robbers after the end of the Old Kingdom and sealed and then reopened more than once until Strabo's door was added. He adds: "If this highly speculative surmise be correct, it is also necessary to assume either that the existence of the door was forgotten or that the entrance was again blocked with facing stones", in order to explain why al-Ma'mun could not find the entrance. Scholars such as Gaston Maspero and Flinders Petrie have noted that evidence for a similar door has been found at the Bent Pyramid of Dashur.

Herodotus visited Egypt in the 5th century BC and recounts a story that he was told concerning vaults under the pyramid built on an island where the body of Khufu lies. Edwards notes that the pyramid had "almost certainly been opened and its contents plundered long before the time of Herodotus" and that it might have been closed again during the Twenty-sixth Dynasty of Egypt when other monuments were restored. He suggests that the story told to Herodotus could have been the result of almost two centuries of telling and retelling by pyramid guides.

9 798885 551618

Printed by Libri Plureos GmbH in Hamburg,
Germany